CITY CYCLING
LOS ANGELES

Text by Kelton Wright
Illustrations by Kelly Carpenter

Rapha.

Thames & Hudson

Original concept created by
Andrew Edwards and Max Leonard

Thanks to my husband,
Ben Foster

City Cycling Los Angeles © 2018 Thames & Hudson Ltd, London

Designed by Michael Lenz, Draught Associates

Illustrations by Kelly Carpenter

First published in 2017 in the United States of America by
Thames & Hudson Inc., 500 Fifth Avenue, New York, New York 10110

www.thamesandhudsonusa.com

Library of Congress Control Number 2017942159

ISBN 978-0-500-29308-9

Printed and bound in China by Everbest Printing Co. Ltd

CONTENTS

HOW TO USE THIS GUIDE

This Los Angeles volume of the *City Cycling* series is designed to give you the confidence to explore the city by bike at your own pace. On the front flaps is a locator map of the whole city to help you orient yourself. Here, you will see five neighbourhoods to explore: Venice, Santa Monica and Malibu (p. 10); Beverly Hills and Hollywood (p. 16); Downtown LA (p. 22); Los Feliz and Echo Park (p. 28); and Pasadena and the Rose Bowl (p. 34).

Each of these neighbourhoods is easily accessible by bike, and is full of cafés, bars, galleries, museums, shops and parks. All are mapped in detail, and our recommendations for places of interest and where to fuel up on coffee and cake, as well as where to find a WiFi connection, are marked. Take a pootle round on your bike and see what suits you.

If you fancy a set itinerary, turn to A Day On The Bike on the front flaps. It takes you on a relaxed 39-km (24-mile) route through some of those parts of Los Angeles we haven't featured in the neighbourhood sections, and visits a few of the more touristy sights. Pick and choose the bits you fancy, go from back to front, and use the route as you wish.

A section on Racing and Training (p. 40) fills you in on some of LA's cycling heritage and provides ideas for longer rides if you want to explore the beautiful countryside around the city. Essential Bike Info (p. 44) discusses road etiquette and the ins and outs of using the cycle-hire scheme and public transportation. And lastly, Links and Addresses (p. 48) will give you the practical details you need to know.

LOS ANGELES: THE CYCLING CITY

Los Angeles, the City of Angels, is known for three things: Hollywood glamour, surfer-friendly beaches and traffic. But that congestion is also why LA is well on its way to becoming a cycling mecca. Riding a bike around the city is often faster than driving. Going from the westside to the eastside can take over two hours in rush-hour traffic, but it's fewer than 32 km (20 miles) from Santa Monica Pier to the eastside neighbourhoods of Los Feliz and Echo Park. People often complain there are more cars than people in LA, but the resurgence of cycling in the city is trying to change that.

All you need to do is drive along the Pacific Coast Highway on a weekend morning to see how popular cycling has become in Los Angeles. Weekend warriors and pros alike train along the Malibu stretch, which offers one canyon climb after another into the Santa Monica Mountains. The tongue-in-cheek hashtag #LAsucksforcycling shows the wide variety of views and climbs available in and around greater Los Angeles. There is no shortage of impressive escapes here. Cycling culture has exploded in this city of pavement and palms, and Los Angeles has recently endorsed a sweeping policy of changes in favour of cyclists called the Mobility Plan 2035. The scheme will add more lanes for bikes and buses on some of the busiest boulevards, leaving less space for cars on some. The intention is to improve safety for pedestrians and cyclists alike in order to lure people out of their cars.

The city wasn't always so car-focused. In the early 20th century, bicycle culture was huge in the City of Angels, with elevated bicycle highways being a favourite attraction. It didn't hurt that LA had the perfect weather for year-round cycling with its dry Mediterranean climate. Angelenos rarely check the weather: nearly every day of the year is sunny and temperate, excluding a few very hot days in August and September and a few rainy ones in January. But as the population swelled by thousands in the 1910s and '20s, so did a flourishing middle class, all keen on owning an automobile in the mild climate and already sweeping community. Today, Los Angeles County is home to over 10 million people and more than 7 million vehicles.

But in the city centre, you'll see more and more people commuting by bike as green bike lanes are painted on the streets, bike-share schemes pop up around the city and former car lanes are converted to bike lanes. Plus, the best parts of LA can often be missed by car. Elevated freeways connecting major hubs to one another can miss the charm of the neighbourhood streets, lined with palm trees, below. Los Angeles's architecture is characterized by low-rise buildings, so there's always a view of blue skies and mountainous peaks, with the Santa Monica Mountains to the north and the San Gabriel Mountains to the east.

To catch the best views of the sky and the city, take your time climbing up to the Griffith Observatory – go at night to see the stars, but go during the day to see the Hollywood sign in all its glory. And for a flat ride with a never-ending stretch of the Pacific Ocean guiding you, look no further than the Marvin Braude Bike Trail, a 35 km (22 mile)-long paved bicycle path running along the shoreline. Or try to catch one of the CicLAvia events, held every few months, during which streets in a part of the city are closed to cars for a day and operate as a public park.

Look to other cyclists to see how things are done in LA, but always remember that the car is still king and abide by the rules of the road. You'll find the cyclists as varied as the suburbs they live in, with beach cruisers on the westside, fixies on the eastside and roadies climbing out of every canyon. Keep your wits about you, and you'll see a diverse city full of glamour, grit and bicycles.

NEIGHBOURHOODS

VENICE, SANTA MONICA & MALIBU

FOR SURFERS, HIPPIES AND FOODIES

The westside of LA, once characterized by sun-bleached surfers and flower children in vans, still maintains its hippie-chic look, but for quite a pretty penny. The communities of Venice, Santa Monica and Malibu line the coast of the greater Los Angeles area, going from trendy to bougie to exclusive in the span of 32 km (20 miles). The westside is a great place for photo-ops, California cuisine, sunset cocktails and people-watching.

Which neighbourhoods comprise the westside of LA is up for debate, but for our purposes, we'll be talking about Venice, Santa Monica, Brentwood, the Pacific Palisades and Malibu. (Santa Monica and Malibu are actually their own cities, but are still lumped into the wider region.) To the south, you'll find the communities of Marina Del Rey, Playa Vista and Playa Del Rey, before hitting the Los Angeles International Airport; further inland are Mar Vista, Culver City and West LA/Westwood. Lines are not finely drawn here, with freeways being referenced as divider lines more frequently than actual municipal delineations, and the westside is often referred to as 'everything west of the 405'.

Let's say you start in Venice. Venice was actually modelled on the Italian city, intended as a beautiful tourist destination of casinos and pier attractions. It fell into disrepair during the Great Depression, but was brought back to life by the Beats and, later, the hippies, as a place for jazz, poetry, art and free love. You'll still find some of the original vision of Venice along the manmade **Venice Canals ❶**, but be prepared to dismount: bikes are prohibited and the residents are not afraid to remind you of that. Vegan restaurants, skyrocketing rents and the Silicon Beach move-in are slowly replacing free love and art, but Venice is still home to westside artistry. The buildings are covered with murals, and the Venice Beach Boardwalk is home to more oddities than the whole of New York.

Start in Venice on Abbot Kinney Blvd, named after the man who built the canals. You'll find perfect brews at **Intelligentsia Coffee ❷** and **Blue Bottle Coffee ❸**, and leave some time to window shop, as there are a slew of galleries and shops always popping up on Abbot Kinney. A visit to the **Tortoise General Store ❹** is a must, if only for the Zen atmosphere and choice of interesting gifts. For a quick bite, stop into **Lemonade ❺**, and for the full dining experience try **Tasting Kitchen ❻**. If you find yourself on Abbot Kinney on the first Friday of the month, save your appetite and join the crowds along this street flocking to the variety of food trucks parked there for First Fridays.

When you're done perusing the boutiques, take Abbot Kinney all the way to the **Venice Beach Boardwalk** ❼, where you'll find street performers of every variety, minimal clothing and the wafting of pinecones and peanut butter from the many medical marijuana dispensaries. There's no better place in LA to get a kitschy souvenir than the boardwalk. Come up from the beach along Rose Ave, being sure not to miss the sculpture on the **Venice Renaissance Building** ❽ at the corner of Rose Ave and Main St – or do miss it if clowns aren't your thing, as this sculpture is a 9 m (30 ft)-high figurine of a ballerina clown.

You'll also find local hotspot **Rose Cafe** ❾ on this corner. It's lost a bit of its old-school charm after a recent renovation, but the food remains top-notch, if the place itself is a little hard to navigate. Also in the area is **Gjusta** ❿: grab a number, order a 'Risky Biscuit' and a *cortado*, and eavesdrop on the local Silicon Beach gossip on the back patio. Further up Rose Ave, opt for full immersion into LA culture by taking away an exorbitantly priced juice from **Moon Juice** ⓫ and order anything at **Café Gratitude** ⓬, where the dishes are all adjectives and you order by saying, 'I am [fill in as necessary].' A sure-fire way to embarrass your friends.

Once you've sampled what Venice has to offer, take either Main St or the beach path to Santa Monica. The pier itself (see also A Day On The Bike) is overrun with tourists, but its history is rich. Wade through the crowds to the end of it to read about just how many times they've had to rebuild it. The original merry-go-round is still there, and there are some pretty steeds to match your bike.

Grab classic beach food and a lemonade at **Hot Dog on a Stick** and watch the gymnasts work out on the rings at the **Original Muscle Beach** . Throughout the summer the pier hosts concerts on Thursdays, and all of Santa Monica picnics on the beach to listen. Skip the 3rd St Promenade (you'll see this anyway on A Day On The Bike): bikes are not allowed and most stores are chains. If your legs are up to it, head further north up to Malibu. Be prepared, however: the beach path ends, and only the most seasoned cyclists ride their bikes on the Pacific Coast Highway.

REFUELLING

FOOD

Flake is the best for a hearty breakfast or lunch

At **Tacos Por Favor** , be sure to try the California burrito for something deliciously unhealthy

DRINK

Dogtown Coffee is a good starting point for a weekend ride

Venice Ale House is a great place to grab a drink and watch the sunset or watch the people

WIFI

TOMS Flagship Store also serves as a café and hangout

SANTA
MONICA
BEACH

SANTA
MONICA
PIER

PALISADES BEACH RD
SANTA MONICA BLVD
BROADWAY
COLORADO AV
OCEAN AVE
PICO BLVD
4TH ST
NEILSON WAY
MAIN ST
OCEAN AVE
OLYMPIC A

1 MILE = 4 MINS
1 KM

BEVERLY HILLS
& HOLLYWOOD

GLAMOUR AND TOURISTS

Beverly Hills and Hollywood, along with their hipper counterpart West Hollywood, make up the film version of Los Angeles, with streets lined with palm trees and immense houses, and movie stars around every corner. But for all the glamour, there's a lot of kitsch, too. You're in tourist-central in this part of town, so look out for aggressive drivers (locals) and clueless drivers (tourists) while on your bike. If you can, bring your climbing legs: it's worth it to explore the Hollywood Hills.

Start in Beverly Hills at the **Larder at Maple Drive ❶**, a little breakfast nook tucked into an inconspicuous office building, and the perfect place to fuel up for a day on your bike. Then amble through the streets just north of Santa Monica Blvd to see some of the city's most glamorous houses, making sure to swing by the spooky **Spadena House ❷**, originally built as a set for silent films. If you're one for photo-ops, ride into the tiny **Beverly Gardens Park ❸** for a picture in front of the Beverly Hills sign. Grab a cheap snack at **Nate 'n Al Delicatessen ❹**, one of the best delis in the city, because you'll need your cash for **Two Rodeo ❺**, the cobblestoned offshoot of Rodeo Dr, lined with Lanvin, Carolina Herrera, Versace, and more. Park your bike, though: riding on the sidewalk here is illegal.

Next up is West Hollywood: not quite as swanky, but lots more fun. West Hollywood is known for its nightlife, but there's more than just partying to do in this part of town. If you're still craving breakfast, head to **Ed's Coffee Shop ❻** for some no-nonsense grub. Or do as the locals do before a big day of exploring and treat yourself to a spa session at **The Gendarmerie ❼**, where a club-like feel caters to all customers. Ride along Melrose Ave for some of the best shopping in the city: whether you're off to a black-tie gala or a late-night rave, you'll find what you're looking for here. Stop into **Decades ❽** for ladies' consignment glamour, or head over to **TenOverSix ❾** for an array of wonderfully kitsch gifts, including chipmunk ornaments and beard oil.

For lunch, head to **Cavatina ❿** and grab a seat on the patio to sit among vine-entwined columns. And you won't want to miss the **Los Angeles County Museum of Art ⓫**. Although it's technically in the Miracle Mile, LACMA is only a couple miles from Melrose Ave and well worth the visit. While you're there, stop by the **La Brea Tar Pits ⓬** for some true tourism. After filling up on culture, any number of places back on Melrose will impress for dinner, but **Fig & Olive ⓭** is a consistent favourite, as is Top Chef winner Michael Voltaggio's **Ink ⓮**. Even if you don't spot the chef, you may spot some other famous faces.

If you, like many of the residents in the neighbourhood, really come alive at night, then Hollywood has everything you need. Recharge with a brew at **Go Get Em Tiger** 🟤15 in Larchmont Village, and if you have a sweet tooth, make sure to try the sweet latte. Incredible food can be found all over this part of town, from fine dining at **Providence** 🟤16 to the casual, twinkling-light charm of **Paru's** 🟤17 to home-cooked Italian meals at **Osteria Mamma** 🟤18.

But more than food, make sure you have an appetite for entertainment, because this is where you'll find it. Catch a movie at the **Hollywood Forever Cemetery** 🟤19, where Cinespia hosts old classics among the tombstones, go to a concert at the **Hollywood Bowl** 🟤20, where there are plenty of bike racks, see a movie at the **TCL Chinese Theatre** 🟤21 on the historic **Hollywood Walk of Fame** 🟤22 or watch stand-up at UCB **Theatre** 🟤23 – the entertainment options are endless. Grab a late-night pizza at **Stella Barra** 🟤24 or order a fried-chicken sandwich at the blink-and-you'll-miss-it window at **Twins Sliders** 🟤25, before finishing off the night at **Good Time's at Davey Wayne's** 🟤26. The name does not lie at this 1970s throwback (rock music and shag carpet included). The most entertaining thing about Hollywood is the people that live there, so wherever you head to, find a perch to people-watch.

REFUELLING

FOOD
Lucques 🟤27 is a classy can't-miss destination for a fancy meal out
Sycamore Kitchen 🟤28 for a lunch worthy of seconds

DRINK
The Pikey 🟤29 is the fanciest pub this side of the pond

WIFI
Paper or Plastik Cafe 🟤30 for the cool and the thirsty

DOWNTOWN LA

Downtown LA is in the middle of its renaissance. No other part of the city has climbed out of decline so quickly to become one of LA's most popular destinations, but be on alert: Skid Row is still an area in need of reform, and crime is still a real problem downtown. Use your best judgment when riding around, and be careful where you lock your bike.

Unlike the rest of the city, Downtown LA operates on a bicycle-friendly and primarily flat grid, where new restaurants and new artists thrive. Whether you're checking out the galleries in the Arts District or chowing down in Chinatown and Little Tokyo, this is the destination for anyone looking to experience a cultural resurgence firsthand. And keep an eye out for the new bike-share scheme: over a thousand bikes were made available in the downtown area in 2016.

Start your day at **Grand Central Market ❶**. This open-air market has been open continuously since 1917, and is the best mix of cultural and nutritional diversity you'll find in the city. If you have the time, wait in the long line of fashionably dressed patrons at **Eggslut ❷** for the pinnacle in egg sandwiches. Next, get your morning fix at **G&B Coffee ❸**, a coffee hotspot that opens to the outside and is the perfect place to caffeinate while keeping an eye on your bike.

If at any point you find yourself needing a tune up, check out **El Maestro Bicycle Shop ❹** for good service and adorable shop pets. On the other side of the market, you'll find the **Bradbury Building ❺**, with its beautiful wood panelling and iron staircases. A must-see for architecture and movie buffs, the city's oldest trademarked building has been featured in films including *Blade Runner*, *Chinatown* and *(500) Days of Summer*. This area has plenty of Art Deco buildings, so keep your eyes peeled.

The next can't-miss building on your list should be the **Walt Disney Concert Hall** ❻, a twisted-metal phenomenon from the mind of Frank Gehry that's worth exploring both inside and out. Across the street, for a different kind of pop culture, you'll find LA's newest contemporary art museum, **The Broad** ❼. Check out over two thousand works of art for free. If contemporary isn't your thing, ride a few blocks over to **El Pueblo de Los Angeles** ❽, the city's original Spanish and Mexican settlement, where the buildings span a century of history and the plaza is filled with flowers and vendors. Grab a *churro* and enjoy the bougainvillea.

For a more substantial meal, make your way through Little Tokyo towards the Arts District, where a new class of creative and professional people have made this the go-to place for hip galleries and great food. Order the three-course lunch special at **Church & State** ❾ for a little bit of Paris in Los Angeles, but make sure to save room for dessert: you're going to want to try the Mexican Chocolate pie at the family-owned café **The Pie Hole** ❿. If a more low-key lunch is what you're looking for, stop in at the industrial-chic **Wurstküche** ⓫ for an elevated sausage experience – or an adventurous one if you're willing to try the rabbit and rattlesnake sausage.

Next up, make your way to **Lot, Stock & Barrel** ⓬ for all the vintage goods you can imagine. It's well curated and very tempting, so come ready to splurge on an investment piece. If you'd rather make an investment piece of your own, check out **Art Share LA** ⓭ to get the creative juices flowing. This warehouse is now 28,000 square feet of studio space including dance and painting studios as well as a gallery and art classrooms. For the culinary artists in you, stop by **Urban Radish** ⓮. It may seem silly to mention a grocery store, but the organic produce, artisan cheeses, and custom brews make this a must stop. Indulge in a bottle of wine and delicious cheese on their patio while you plan your next steps.

Finally, for the night-crowd, check out **The Edison** ⓯. This reformed power plant is a scene every night with DJs, live bands and handcrafted cocktails. Look smart here to look part of the crowd while enjoying silent-video montages projected on the Art Deco-chic walls.

REFUELLING

FOOD
Head to **B.S. Taqueria** ⓰ for life-changing tacos
Bestia ⓱ is a great place to load up on carbs before biking the city again

DRINK
Cafe Demitasse ⓲ for Japanese-style cold brew
Far Bar ⓳ for every kind of whisky you could wish for, plus wasabi fries

WIFI
The Springs ⓴ is a workspace, yoga studio, juice bar and restaurant – and every bit LA

LOS FELIZ
& ECHO PARK

THE COOL AND THE VINTAGE

Nowhere in the city will you find more artisan goods, beards or coffee shops than in the eastside. But the coolest neighbourhoods in LA are cool for a reason: check out this part of town for great affordable eats, rare goods and the best places to hang out for a while. Tourists don't always head this way, so prepare to hang with the locals and eat like them, too.

Starting in Los Feliz, you'll find the perfect on-the-go snack at both **Cafe Los Feliz ❶** for flaky croissants or **HomeState ❷** for delicious breakfast tacos and plenty of space to sit outside with your bike. After breakfast be sure to ride into Griffith Park, where you'll find the **Greek Theatre ❸**, the **LA Zoo ❹**, the **Griffith Observatory ❺** and a 14-km (9-mile) tree-lined bike loop. You'll also see plenty of roadies in kit hammering their way up on the weekends. Hire bikes are available at **Spokes 'n Stuff ❻** if you're without your own set of wheels.

Back down in Los Feliz, if you're craving a snack, stop into **Little Dom's ❼** at the top of Hillhurst Ave and grab something from the deli to-go counter. Keep an eye out for celebrities, too. After that, check out local landmark **Soap Plant / Wacko ❽** (or just Wacko's, to the locals) for a trip back to the '70s. The store is a favourite of hippies and punks looking for posters, taxidermy, action figures, and more. And make sure to swing by **Skylight Books ❾**, one of the city's best independent bookstores, chock-full of local authors, 'zines and graphic novels. One you've gotten your literary fill, be prepared to spend some time popping in and out of shops in Sunset Junction, the downtown area of Silver Lake.

First up, head over to the **Mohawk General Store ❿** for goods from the likes of Dries Van Noten and Acne, but save some cash for **ReForm School ⓫**, where you'll find some of the neatest trinkets and keepsakes this side of the 405. Up next is **Le Pink ⓬**, the local apothecary with all kinds of candles, soaps, and other essentials for the good life. Don't miss **Spice Station ⓭** or **Vacation Vinyl ⓮** either: the names speak for themselves.

When you get hungry, there are some great options in the 'hood. Try out **Pine & Crane** ⑮, a sweet Taiwanese eatery, and order your meal to go, so you can enjoy it outside in the picnic area with your bike. Or for a farm-fresh approach, wait in the line at **Sqirl** ⑯ for the best ricotta on brioche you're likely to find. Some of the best Thai food can be found at **Night + Market Song** ⑰; make sure to try the 'Startled Pig' for a strong kick to the tastebuds. If you're ready to load up on carbohydrates for tomorrow's ride, don't miss **Alimento** ⑱, a *Bon Appetit* favourite, where the tortellini *in brodo* is a can't-miss.

Another can't-miss is **Golden Saddle Cyclery** ⑲ (see also p. 42). It's a regular hangout for local cyclists, not just because of the small-batch cold brew, but also because of the great service and friendly staff. This is the place to get tips on local rides and food, and you'll see many of their customers every Wednesday morning from 7 to 8am partaking in **LA River Camp Coffee** ⑳, along the bike path at Sunnynook River Park. BYO coffee and say hello. If cafés are more your thing, you can't go wrong finishing a ride at **Proof Bakery** ㉑ for one of their ham and cheese croissants, or at **Broome St General Store** ㉒. If you stop at the latter, make sure to check out the **Chandelier Tree** ㉓ nearby: an odd and worthy sight.

For a different kind of pedalling, try your hand at romance and take a pedal boat out on to **Echo Park Lake** ㉔. You'll be treated to great views of downtown, and if you stop at **Square One at the Boathouse** ㉕, you can treat yourself to a great snack. **Ostrich Farm** ㉖ is a homey place that's good for a family meal or a date; especially noteworthy is their delicious pot pie. If something a little sexier is on the menu, try **The Semi-Tropic** ㉗, where the jungle decor and leather sofas really live up to the name.

REFUELLING

FOOD	DRINK
Barbrix ㉘ for when you just want some good cheese and good wine	**Dresden Room** ㉙ ('the Den') for live jazz **Bar Covell** ㉚ for your inner wine buff

WIFI
Caffe Vita ㉛ is a good place to tap away and sip on fresh mint tea
H Coffee House ㉜ for caffeine in a Craftsman-style converted home

GRIFFITH PARK

ROOSEVELT
GOLF COURSE

LOS FELIZ AV

LOS FELIZ AV

LOS FELIZ AV

ROWENA AV

LOS FELIZ

FRANKLIN AV

FRANKLIN AV

PROSPECT AV

SILVER LAKE

HOLLYWOOD BLVD

BARNSDALL
ART PARK

HOLLYWOOD BLVD

SUNSET BLVD

FOUNTAIN AV

FOUNTAIN AV

SANTA MONICA BLVD

SANTA MONICA BLVD

LA CITY
COLLEGE

BICYCLE DISTRICT

MELROSE AV

MELROSE AV

OAKWOOD AV

BEVERLY BLVD

KOREATOWN

W TEMPLE ST

101

RESERVOIR ST

SUNSET BLVD

SILVER LAKE BLVD

BEVERLY BLVD

1 MILE = 4 MINS

1 KM

W 3RD ST

W 3RD ST

W 3RD ST

N NORMANDIE AV

N VERMONT AV

N HILLHURST AV

ST GEORGE ST

HYPERION AV

GRIFFITH PARK BLVD

N VIRGIL ST

N HOOVER ST

SILVER LAKE BLVD

N BENTON WAY

N CORONADO ST

S VIRGIL AV

7

1

9

29

32

8

2

30

31

22

23

28

10

11

14

13

19

12

15

18

17

16

20

PASADENA &
THE ROSE BOWL

GARDENS AND ROSES AND ARTS AND CRAFTS

If you're looking for green and charm, you'll find them both on this side of town. Pasadena's rolling landscape makes for punchy climbs for the roadies and beautiful scenery for everyone else. Try to hit the area in the springtime, when the lilac is in bloom. Its old-money past can be seen in the mansions, museums and gardens, but new life has also sprung up in restaurants and shops, and all of it is worth seeing.

When riding around Pasadena, your most important can't-miss is the **Rose Bowl ❶**. Known nationally for its annual college-football game, it's known locally as a ride favourite of cyclists. Be careful where you ride, though: they're serious here about where bikes are allowed and where they are not. And don't forget to check out the Rose Bowl Flea Market on the second Sunday of the month for some great finds. Just south of here you'll find yourself in **Brookside Park ❷**, 62 acres of green space with a biking trail that flanks its entire east side. If you've come with little ones, the **Kidspace Children's Museum ❸** is the least painful of the children's museums, with plenty of space to sit back and relax.

For a caffeine fix, if you're in a hurry stop by **Copa Vida ❹**. It operates on an honour system, and you can pour your own for about £1.60 ($2). If you'd rather sit down and linger, try **Lavender & Honey Espresso Bar ❺**. Grab a seat outside, and enjoy the delicious peanut butter/honey/banana toast. To satisfy your shopping needs, head down Colorado Blvd, through the heart of Pasadena. Stop into **Indiana Colony ❻**, Pasadena's relaxed answer to the Grand Central Market (p. 22), for something decadent from **Coolhaus ❼** or healthy from **Pressed Juicery ❽**. Around the corner, **Gold Bug ❾** sells funky gifts and oddities, like chandeliers made of emu eggs. Idle down to **Vroman's Bookstore ❿** – this giant bookstore is over 100 years old and is always hosting literary events.

When you're all shopped out, it's time to take in the architecture. Walk through the rose-filled courtyard of **Pasadena City Hall ⓫** and make your way to **Castle Green ⓬** for a dose of old Hollywood glamour. For Arts and Crafts architecture, head over to the **Gamble House ⓭**, where tours are led Thursday–Sunday. Be sure to ride through Old Pasadena, a historic district where many movies were filmed, and **Bungalow Heaven ⓮**, a 16-block area filled with Arts and Crafts bungalows. For a pick-me-up, stop into **POP Champagne and Dessert Bar ⓯** for truffle mac-and-cheese bites. A more substantial lunch can be found at **Pie'n Burger ⓰**, where you'll find – you guessed it – old-fashioned burgers, or grab a brew at **La Grande Orange Cafe ⓱** in a converted 1930s train depot.

Then head down to South Pasadena to check out the old town and **Arlington Garden** ⓲, home to plenty of drought-tolerant plants (important for this neck of the woods). For bike goodies, stop by the affectionately named **Cub House** ⓳ to stock up on bottles, caps and more. Then – if you've got any energy left – it's time for a visit to the **Huntington Library, Art Gallery and Botanical Gardens** ⓴, where you could spend a whole day exploring the grounds and collections.

Fill up on dinner at **Abricott** ㉑ for Asian-fusion cuisine in a restaurant that looks and feels more like a coffee shop, or try the farmers' market-driven food at **Union** ㉒. Either option will leave you satisfied. Finish the day at **Lucky Baldwin's** ㉓ for a beer in very British surroundings, or **1886 Bar** ㉔ for a delicious cocktail. A low-key day, finished off with a low-key end.

REFUELLING

FOOD
Luggage Room Pizzeria ㉕ for pizza in a former station luggage-collection room
Dots Cupcakes ㉖ for chocolate cupcakes with peanut-butter frosting

DRINK
Euro Pane Bakery ㉗ for delicious hot chocolate at a tiny neighbourhood joint
Kings Row Gastropub ㉘ for a brew with burgers and chips

WIFI
Home Brewed Bar ㉙ is a sunny space with a good working atmosphere

RACING & TRAINING

Los Angeles is a climber's dream, with the Pacific Coast Highway offering sea-level access to more than a dozen climbs into the Santa Monica Mountains, most of which interconnect with each other. These canyons not only offer sweeping views of the ocean and the city, but also an escape from the congestion in the basin below. Permits for races in the mountains are hard to come by – the area is very wealthy and road cycling is not popular enough in the States to close the roads. But the dreamy climbs and descents still provide a fertile, year-round training ground for pros and amateurs alike.

Even without a full calendar of races, Los Angeles has still managed to create a name for itself in the history of cycling. Both the 1932 and 1984 Olympic Games landed in Los Angeles. In 1932, a velodrome was installed inside Pasadena's Rose Bowl (see also p. 35) for the track cycling events, and in 1984 a new facility was built in Carson. This later iteration was demolished in 2003, making way for the **VELO Sports Center,** which remains the only Olympic-standard velodrome in the US. The 1984 Olympics were also the first to include women's events, where American Connie Carpenter-Phinney took the gold in the road race. It was arguably the best year for USA Cycling, with the team taking home nine medals.

The most notable race in recent years to take place in Los Angeles actually finished here: the **Tour of California**, in 2015. The Rose Bowl acted as the finish line, with international superstar Peter Sagan taking the yellow jersey in general classification, and Mark Cavendish the green jersey in sprint classification.

Though road races may not be frequent in Los Angeles proper, club rides certainly are. You're likely to find one any day of the week on both sides of the city. For a flat, circuit-type ride, there are two popular options: on the westside, you can join up with riders on the **New Pier Ride** (or NPR), as they do laps at the Westchester Parkway by the airport. The ride leaves from the Manhattan Beach Pier every Tuesday and Thursday at 6:40am. On the eastside, you can join one of the longest-standing group rides in the States: the **Rose Bowl Ride**. For over 60 years, cyclists have been meeting here just before 6pm on Tuesdays and Thursdays to do laps around the Rose Bowl. But remember, this is a destination for more than just cyclists. Look out for cars, runners, strollers, and the like.

If climbing is your thing, join the **Velo Club La Grange** every Sunday morning as they race up Nichols Canyon. Both conversation and riders tend to peter out on approaching 'The Wall', the final 100 m (328 ft), where the wrong gear choice will leave you in the dust. If you're visiting between November and February, join the club's Simi Ride on Saturdays at 8:30am on the corner of Alscot and Los Angeles Ave in Simi Valley. This ride blossoms in distance, speed and riders as the off-season nears its end. For those looking for hill intervals, the club meets at 6:30am on Thursdays on the corner of 26th St and San Vicente Blvd in Santa Monica for laps up and around the twisting Amalfi Dr neighbourhood. Beautiful streets, minimal traffic and big houses make for great scenery to accompany the suffering.

For every planned group ride, there are 10 other mini-pelotons of friends and allies making use of LA's training ground. There are great roads to try in every part of the city. On the eastside, try Highway 2, the road to Mt Baldy, and Glendora Mountain Rd (known by locals simply as GMR). For the truly fit (not just on pavement, but on gravel and dirt), try the **Mt Lowe Railway Trail** for incredible views and stamina. For those in the Beverly Hills/Hollywood area, Franklin Canyon and Benedict Canyon connect to Mulholland Dr for classic sweeping views of the city on either side of the ridge. And if you find yourself on the westside, try the Topanga Canyon climb. Halfway up, you'll find yourself in the old hippie refuge of Topanga: unincorporated, and proud of it. Stay to the right past town to stop in at **Topanga Creek Bicycles** (see also p. 46) for serve-yourself banana bread.

Finally, if you're looking for a shop to outfit you or tune up your bike, there are great options on both sides of the city. On the eastside, stop in **Golden Saddle Cyclery** (see also p. 30) in Silver Lake. Whether you need kit, a tune-up or a low-down on what's good in the neighbourhood, this is the place to go. On the westside, you'll be taken care of at **Bike Effect** in Santa Monica. If you're shipping your bike, this is a great place to have it shipped to and rebuilt for when you arrive in the city. Service is top-notch, and so are the free drinks.

ESSENTIAL BIKE INFO

Cycling is just coming into vogue in LA, so it's worth remembering that the car still reigns supreme here. You'll still find a healthy mix of beach cruisers in the city and pros on the beach path, but it's best to research routes ahead of time to check for bike lanes and traffic, in case of cars speeding on your left and doors opening on your right.

ETIQUETTE

Like in any big city, you'll find all types of cyclists in LA, from strict law-abiders to crosswalk-jumpers. Here are a few tips to keep you in the good graces of both drivers and cyclists:

- Never assume a car has seen you. Many drivers in LA are checking their mirrors to look at themselves, not you.
- The fine for jumping a red light is hefty, and tickets are not rare. Wait for green. Turning right on red is acceptable, however – just check for pedestrians first.
- It's illegal in many parts of LA to ride your bike on the sidewalk.
- Do not pass other cyclists on the right. Go around them as you would if overtaking in a car.
- Getting 'doored' is not uncommon. Even if there is a bike lane, do not assume the cars parked next to it are checking for you.
- Signal frequently to cars and other cyclists to indicate what you're doing. Cars are not used to cyclists here and often make erratic and poor decisions around them because of this.

SAFETY

LA is not littered with bike paths, but the sight of a cyclist is becoming more and more common. So long as you avoid the main boulevards during high traffic, you should find cycling relatively safe here. Here are some additional safety tips when facing the roads:

- Side streets in LA usually have stop signs at every block. While many cyclists breeze through them on low traffic roads, remember that cars often do, too.

- Drivers are notoriously aggressive in LA. Always defer to the more cautious action, and stay out of blind spots.
- 'Taking the lane' is legal in LA, meaning when a lane is too narrow to safely share side by side with a motor vehicle, you can prevent unsafe passing by riding near the centre of the lane. Drivers are often not fans of this manoeuvre, but it is legal, and it is safer.
- If you use headphones while riding, only use one. It's illegal to wear earplugs in both ears, or to have a headset that covers both ears.
- You'll see 'Bike Route' signs posted around the city – these are not reliable for following a route, nor are those roads treated any differently by drivers.
- If it's raining, be very careful. Rain or any kind of weather is rare in LA, so accidents with vehicles are more frequent when it's wet.
- Use extra caution when riding on the beach paths. Novices rent many of the bikes you'll see there and sandy conditions make for some wobbly newbies.

SECURITY

Bike theft is common in LA, and bike skeletons can be found chained up to many street signs and bike racks. Do not leave any bike unlocked and unattended, and take your cues from local cyclists: if no one else is locking their bike in a certain area, don't lock yours there either. Think about using two locks and securing the wheels so that thieves may pick an easier target. Seats, pumps, saddlebags, and so on are all at risk in LA, so it's unadvised to leave your bike locked up outside overnight. Highest-risk areas are in the coastal communities, so if you're looking to enjoy the beach, take your bike with you.

FINDING YOUR WAY

While much of LA runs on a grid, there's no consistent naming system or continuity to make it easy to follow. Communities like Santa Monica and Beverly Hills are not actually part of Los Angeles, making it even more complicated. The green 'Bike Route' signs appear and disappear at their leisure, and bike lanes end with little or no warning. The best way to get around LA by bike is to plan your route ahead of time and follow the road signs. Roads are clearly marked at nearly every intersection. Landmarks that can help you understand the lay of the land are the Santa Monica Mountains, the San Gabriel Mountains and the Pacific Ocean.

But beware of trying to navigate by placing the ocean to the west and the San Gabriel Mountains to the east. The city does not lie on a north–south-east–west grid, even though many people refer to it that way. Carry a map.

CITY BIKES AND BIKE HIRE

Santa Monica is currently the only city in Los Angeles County with a bike-share scheme, offering 500 bikes at 80 locations within Santa Monica for about £4.80 ($6) per hour. You can reserve bikes with **Breeze Bike Share** through the **Social Bicycle** app, but prepare to stand out: the bikes are lime-green and covered in logos for Hulu. **LA Metro** also launched a bike-share scheme in Downtown LA in 2016, offering nearly 1,100 bicycles at over 60 bike-share stations for a fee of about £2.80 ($3.50) per 30 minutes.

For bike hire, you'll find a myriad of places along the beach (most only accept cash, so be prepared). If looking inland, check out **Just Ride LA** in downtown. For a road bike, call **Helen's Cycles** in advance to reserve one from their selection. For an electric bike, try **Pedal or Not**. For a mountain bike, head to **Topanga Creek Bicycles** (see also p. 42) in Topanga Canyon. The Santa Monica Mountains are riddled with great fire roads for anyone looking for some easy dirt miles.

OTHER PUBLIC TRANSPORT

Los Angeles is not known for its public transportation, but a few options are available. Most of the city is accessible by bus, though it can take hours in traffic to cross the city this way. Metro buses have space for two bicycles on the front rack. Be advised, you cannot lock your bike to the rack, so sit near the front of the bus to keep an eye on your bike.

Bikes are also welcome on all Metro trains without any additional fee. There are marked areas on the carriages for where to enter with your bike and where to stand. All rail stations have bike racks, with some offering bike lockers. Certain stations, like Hollywood and Vine and Culver City, will be introducing **Bike Hubs** in 2017 with secure parking, onsite mechanics and bike parts. The Metro system is growing in Los Angeles, but coverage of the city is still limited.

Taxis can be hard to come by in Los Angeles, and very few will take bikes. If you find yourself stranded, your best bet will be to download a ride-share app like **Uber** or **Lyft** and request a larger car.

TRAVELLING TO LA WITH BIKES

If you are travelling internationally to Los Angeles with a bike, be prepared to pay upwards of around £240 ($300) round trip to check a bike on the plane. Smaller airlines like Southwest, JetBlue and Frontier offer lower prices than the larger airlines, but fees still add up. Despite only being 11 km (7 miles) from Venice, it is not advisable to bike to or from **Los Angeles International Airport**, so remember to arrange transport to the airport that has room for your bike.

LINKS & ADDRESSES

1886 BAR
1250 S Fair Oaks Ave,
Pasadena, CA 91105
theraymond.com

3RD ST PROMENADE
1351 3rd Street Promenade, #201,
Santa Monica, CA 90401
3rdstreetpromenade.com

ABRICOTT
238 S Lake Ave,
Pasadena, CA 91101
abricott.com

ALIMENTO
1710 Silver Lake Blvd,
Los Angeles, CA 90026
alimentola.com

ARLINGTON GARDEN
275 Arlington Dr,
Pasadena, CA 91105
arlingtongardeninpasadena.org

ART SHARE LA
801 E 4th Pl,
Los Angeles, CA 90013
artsharela.org

BAR COVELL
4628 Hollywood Blvd,
Los Angeles, CA 90027
barcovell.com

BARBRIX
2442 Hyperion Ave,
Los Angeles, CA 90027
barbrix.com

BESTIA
2121 E 7th Pl,
Los Angeles, CA 90021
bestiala.com

BEVERLY GARDENS PARK
N Santa Monica Blvd,
Beverly Hills, CA 90210
beverlyhills.org

BEVERLY HILTON
9876 Wilshire Blvd,
Beverly Hills, CA 90210
beverlyhilton.com

BLUE BOTTLE COFFEE
1103 Abbot Kinney Blvd,
Venice, CA 90291
bluebottlecoffee.com

BLUE PLATE TACO
1515 Ocean Ave,
Santa Monica, CA 90401
blueplatesantamonica.com

BRADBURY BUILDING
304 S Broadway,
Los Angeles, CA 90013

BRENTWOOD COUNTRY MART
225 26th St,
Santa Monica, CA 90402
brentwoodcountrymart.com

BROOME ST GENERAL STORE
2912 Rowena Ave,
Los Angeles, CA 90039
broomestgeneral.com

B.S. TAQUERIA
514 W 7th St,
Los Angeles, CA 90014
bstaqueria.com

BUNGALOW HEAVEN
Pasadena, CA 91104
bungalowheaven.org

CAFE DEMITASSE
135 S San Pedro St,
Los Angeles, CA 90012
cafedemitasse.com

CAFÉ GRATITUDE
512 Rose Ave,
Venice, CA 90291
cafegratitude.com

CAFE LOS FELIZ
2118 Hillhurst Ave,
Los Angeles, CA 90027

CAFFE LUXXE
225 26th St,
Santa Monica, CA 90402
caffeluxxe.com

CAFFE VITA
4459 Sunset Blvd,
Los Angeles, CA 90027
caffevita.com

CASTLE GREEN
99 S Raymond Ave,
Pasadena, CA 91105
castlegreen.com

CAVATINA
1200 Alta Loma Rd,
West Hollywood, CA 90069
cavatinala.com

CHANDELIER TREE
2811 W Silver Lake Dr,
Los Angeles, CA 90039

CHATEAU MARMONT
8221 Sunset Blvd,
Los Angeles, CA 90046
chateaumarmont.com

CHEZ JAY
1657 Ocean Ave,
Santa Monica, CA 90401
chezjays.com

CHURCH & STATE
1850 Industrial St,
Los Angeles, CA 90021
churchandstatebistro.com

CINERAMA DOME
6360 Sunset Blvd,
Los Angeles, CA 90028
arclightcinemas.com

COOLHAUS
59 E Colorado Blvd,
Pasadena, CA 91103
eatcoolhaus.com

COPA VIDA
70 S Raymond Ave,
Pasadena, CA 91105
copa-vida.com

DECADES
8214 Melrose Ave,
Los Angeles, CA 90046
decadesinc.com

DOGTOWN COFFEE
2003 Main St,
Santa Monica, CA 90405
dogtowncoffee.com

DOTS CUPCAKES
21 N Fair Oaks Ave,
Pasadena, CA 91103
dotscupcakes.com

DRESDEN ROOM
1760 N Vermont Ave,
Los Angeles, CA 90027
thedresden.com

ECHO PARK LAKE
751 Echo Park Ave,
Los Angeles, CA 90026
laparks.org/aquatic/lake/echo-
park-lake

ED'S COFFEE SHOP
460 N Robertson Blvd,
West Hollywood, CA 90048
facebook.com/pages/
Eds-Coffee-Shop

EGGSLUT
Grand Central Market,
317 S Broadway,
Los Angeles, CA 90013
eggslut.com

EL PUEBLO DE LOS ANGELES
125 Paseo De La Plaza,
Los Angeles, CA 90012
elpueblo.lacity.org

EURO PANE BAKERY
950 E Colorado Blvd,
Pasadena, CA 91106

EVELEIGH
8752 Sunset Blvd,
Los Angeles, CA 90069
theeveleigh.com

FAR BAR
347 E 1st St,
Los Angeles, CA 90012
farbarla.com

FIG & OLIVE
8490 Melrose Pl,
West Hollywood, CA 90069
figandolive.com

FIRST FRIDAYS
abbotkinneyfirstfridays.com

FLAKE
513 Rose Ave,
Venice, CA 90291
veniceflake.com

G&B COFFEE
Grand Central Market,
317 S Broadway,
Los Angeles, CA 90013
gandbcoffee.com

GAMBLE HOUSE
4 Westmoreland Pl,
Pasadena, CA 91103
gamblehouse.org

GJUSTA
320 Sunset Ave,
Venice, CA 90291
gjusta.com

GO GET EM TIGER
230 N Larchmont Blvd,
Los Angeles, CA 90004
ggetla.com

GOLD BUG
22 E Union St,
Pasadena, CA 91103
goldbugpasadena.com

**GOOD TIME'S AT DAVEY
WAYNE'S**
1611 N El Centro Ave,
Los Angeles, CA 90028
goodtimesatdaveywaynes.com

GRAND CENTRAL MARKET
317 S Broadway,
Los Angeles, CA 90013
grandcentralmarket.com

GREEK THEATRE
2700 N Vermont Ave,
Los Angeles, CA 90027
greektheatrela.com

GRIFFITH OBSERVATORY
2800 E Observatory Rd,
Los Angeles, CA 90027
griffithobservatory.org

H COFFEE HOUSE
1750 Hillhurst Ave,
Los Angeles, CA 90027
hcoffeehousela.com

HOLLYWOOD BOWL
2301 Highland Ave,
Los Angeles, CA 90068
hollywoodbowl.com

**HOLLYWOOD FOREVER
CEMETERY**
6000 Santa Monica Blvd,
Los Angeles, CA 90038
hollywoodforever.com

HOLLYWOOD WALK OF FAME
7018 Hollywood Blvd,
Los Angeles, CA 90028
walkoffame.com

HOME BREWED BAR
39 N Arroyo Pkwy,
Pasadena, CA 91103
homebrewedbar.com

HOMESTATE
4624 Hollywood Blvd,
Los Angeles, CA 90027
myhomestate.com

HOT DOG ON A STICK
1633 Ocean Front Walk,
Santa Monica, CA 90401
hotdogonastick.com

HOTEL SHANGRI-LA
1301 Ocean Ave,
Santa Monica, CA 90401
shangrila-hotel.com

**HUNTINGTON LIBRARY,
ART GALLERY AND
BOTANICAL GARDENS**
1151 Oxford Rd,
San Marino, CA 91108
huntington.org

INDIANA COLONY
59 E Colorado Blvd,
Pasadena, CA 91105

INK
8360 Melrose Ave, #107,
Los Angeles, CA 90069
mvink.com

INTELLIGENTSIA COFFEE
1331 Abbot Kinney Blvd,
Venice, CA 90291
intelligentsiacoffee.com

KIDSPACE CHILDREN'S MUSEUM
480 N Arroyo Blvd,
Pasadena, CA 91103
kidspacemuseum.org

KINGS ROW GASTROPUB
20 E Colorado Blvd,
Pasadena, CA 91103
kingsrowpub.com

LA BREA TAR PITS
5801 Wilshire Blvd,
Los Angeles, CA 90036
tarpits.org

LA GRANDE ORANGE CAFE
260 S Raymond Ave,
Pasadena, CA 91105
lgostationcafe.com

LARDER AT MAPLE DRIVE
345 N Maple Dr,
Beverly Hills, CA 90210
thelarderatmaple.com

LA RIVER CAMP COFFEE
Los Angeles River Bike Path,
Los Angeles, CA 90039

LA ZOO
5333 Zoo Dr,
Los Angeles, CA 90027
lazoo.org

**LAVENDER & HONEY
ESPRESSO BAR**
1383 E Washington Blvd,
Pasadena, CA 91104
lavenderandhoneyespresso.com

LEMONADE
1661 Abbot Kinney Blvd,
Venice, CA 90291
lemonadela.com

LE PINK
3820 Sunset Blvd,
Los Angeles, CA 90026
wlovelepink.com

LITTLE DOM'S
2128 Hillhurst Ave,
Los Angeles, CA 90027
littledoms.com

**LOS ANGELES COUNTY MUSEUM
OF ART**
5905 Wilshire Blvd,
Los Angeles, CA 90036
lacma.org

LOT, STOCK & BARREL
801 ½ Traction Ave.
Los Angeles, CA 90026
lotstockandbarrel.com

LUCKY BALDWIN'S
17 S Raymond Ave,
Pasadena, CA 91105
luckybaldwins.com

LUCQUES
8474 Melrose Ave,
West Hollywood, CA 90069
lucques.com

LUGGAGE ROOM PIZZERIA
260 S Raymond Ave,
Pasadena, CA 91105
theluggageroom.com

MOHAWK GENERAL STORE
4011 Sunset Blvd,
Los Angeles, CA 90029
mohawkgeneralstore.com

MOON JUICE
507 Rose Ave,
Venice, CA 90291
moonjuiceshop.com

NATE 'N AL DELICATESSEN
414 N Beverly Dr,
Beverly Hills, CA 90210
natenal.com

NIGHT + MARKET SONG
3322 Sunset Blvd,
Los Angeles, CA 90026
nightmarketsong.com

ORIGINAL MUSCLE BEACH
Ocean Front Walk,
Santa Monica, CA 90401
musclebeach.net

ORIGINAL PANTRY CAFÉ
877 S Figueroa St,
Los Angeles, CA 90017
pantrycafe.com

OSTERIA MAMMA
5732 Melrose Ave,
Los Angeles, CA 90004
osteriamamma.com

OSTRICH FARM
1525 Sunset Blvd,
Los Angeles, CA 90026
ostrichfarmla.com

PALISADES PARK
Ocean Ave,
Santa Monica, CA 90401
smgov.net

PAPER OR PLASTIK CAFE
5772 W Pico Blvd,
Los Angeles, CA 90019
paperorplastikcafe.com

PARU'S
5140 Sunset Blvd,
Los Angeles, CA 90027
parusrestaurant.com

PASADENA CITY HALL
100 Garfield Ave,
Pasadena, CA 91101
cityofpasadena.net

PIE'N BURGER
913 E California Blvd,
Pasadena, CA 91106
pienburger.com

PINE & CRANE
1521 Griffith Park Blvd,
Los Angeles, CA 90026
pineandcrane.com

**POP CHAMPAGNE AND
DESSERT BAR**
33 E Union St,
Pasadena, CA 91103
popchampagnebar.com

PRESSED JUICERY
59 E Colorado Blvd,
Pasadena, CA 91105
pressedjuicery.com

PROOF BAKERY
3156 Glendale Blvd,
Los Angeles, CA 90039
proofbakeryla.com

PROVIDENCE
5955 Melrose Ave,
Los Angeles, CA 90038
providencela.com

REFORM SCHOOL
3902 Sunset Blvd,
Los Angeles, CA 90029
reformschoolrules.com

ROSE BOWL
1001 Rose Bowl Dr,
Pasadena, CA 91103
rosebowlstadium.com

ROSE CAFE
220 Rose Ave,
Venice, CA 90291
rosecafevenice.com

ROXY THEATRE
9009 Sunset Blvd,
West Hollywood, CA 90069
theroxy.com

SANTA MONICA PIER
200 Santa Monica Pier,
Santa Monica, CA 90401
santamonicapier.org

SANTA MONICA (STATUE)
Palisades Park,
Pacific Coast Hwy,
Santa Monica, CA 90401
publicartinpublicplaces.info

SKYLIGHT BOOKS
1818 N Vermont Ave,
Los Angeles, CA 90027
skylightbooks.com

SOAP PLANT / WACKO
4633 Hollywood Blvd,
Los Angeles, CA 90027
soapplant.com

SPADENA HOUSE
516 Walden Dr,
Beverly Hills, CA 90210
beverlyhills.org

SPICE STATION
3819 Sunset Blvd,
Los Angeles, CA 90026
spicestationsilverlake.com

SQIRL
720 N Virgil Ave,
Los Angeles, CA 90029
squirlla.com

**SQUARE ONE AT THE
BOATHOUSE**
751 Echo Park Ave,
Los Angeles, CA 90026
squareonedining.com/boathouse.php

STELLA BARRA PIZZERIA
6372 Sunset Blvd,
Hollywood, CA 90028
stellabarra.com

SWEET ROSE CREAMERY
225 26th St #51,
Santa Monica, CA 90402
sweetrosecreamery.com

SYCAMORE KITCHEN
143 S La Brea Ave,
Los Angeles, CA 90036
thesycamorekitchen.com

TACOS POR FAVOR
826 Hampton Dr,
Los Angeles, CA 90291
tacosporfavor.net

TASTING KITCHEN
1633 Abbot Kinney Blvd,
Venice, CA 90291
thetastingkitchen.com

TCL CHINESE THEATRE
6801 Hollywood Blvd,
Hollywood, CA 90028
tclchinesetheatres.com

TENOVERSIX
8425 Melrose Ave,
Los Angeles, CA 90069
shop.tenover6.com

THE BROAD
221 S Grand Ave,
Los Angeles, CA 90012
thebroad.org

THE EDISON
108 W 2nd St, #101,
Los Angeles, CA 90012
edisondowntown.com

THE GENDARMERIE
9069 Nemo St,
West Hollywood, CA 90069
thegendarmerie.com

THE MISFIT
225 Santa Monica Blvd,
Santa Monica, CA 90401
themisfitrestaurant.com

THE PIE HOLE
714 Traction Ave,
Los Angeles, CA 90013
thepieholela.com

THE PIKEY
7617 Sunset Blvd,
Los Angeles, CA 90046
thepikeyla.com

THE SEMI-TROPIC
1412 Glendale Blvd,
Los Angeles, CA 90026
thesemitropic.com

THE SPRINGS
608 Mateo St,
Los Angeles, CA 90021
thespringsla.com

TOMS FLAGSHIP STORE
1344 Abbot Kinney Blvd,
Venice, CA 90291
toms.com/venice

TORTOISE GENERAL STORE
1208 Abbot Kinney Blvd,
Venice, CA 90291
tortoisegeneralstore.com

TWINS SLIDERS
5940 Sunset Blvd,
Los Angeles, CA 90028
twinssliders.com

TWO RODEO
9480 Dayton Way,
Beverly Hills, CA 90210
2rodeo.com

UCB THEATRE
5919 Franklin Ave,
Los Angeles, CA 90028
franklin.ucbtheatre.com

UNION
37 E Union St,
Pasadena, CA 91103
unionpasadena.com

URBAN RADISH
661 Imperial St,
Los Angeles, CA 90021
urban-radish.com

VACATION VINYL
3815 Sunset Blvd,
Los Angeles, CA 90026
thejvdasgoat.com

VENICE ALE HOUSE
2 Rose Ave,
Venice, CA 90291
venicealehouse.com

VENICE BEACH BOARDWALK
1800 Ocean Front Walk,
Venice, CA 90291
venicebeach.com

VENICE RENAISSANCE BUILDING
255 Main St,
Venice, CA 90291

VROMAN'S BOOKSTORE
695 E. Colorado Blvd,
Pasadena, CA 91101
vromansbookstore.com

WALT DISNEY CONCERT HALL
111 S Grand Ave,
Los Angeles, CA 90012
laphil.com

WHISKY A GO GO
8901 Sunset Blvd,
West Hollywood, CA 90069
whiskeyagogo.com

WURSTKÜCHE
800 E 3rd St,
Los Angeles, CA 90013
wurstkuche.com

BIKE SHOPS, CLUBS, RACES AND VENUES

BIKE EFFECT
910 Broadway, #100,
Santa Monica, CA 90401
bikeeffect.com

BIKE HUBS
bikehub.com/metro

BREEZE BIKE SHARE
1631 Colorado Ave,
Santa Monica, CA 90404
santamonicabikehsare.com

CICLAVIA
525 S Hewitt St,
Los Angeles, CA 90013
ciclavia.org

CUB HOUSE
1412 El Centro St,
South Pasadena, CA 91030
teamdreambicyclingteam.com

EL MAESTRO BICYCLE SHOP
806 S Main St,
Los Angeles, CA 90014
elmaestrobicycles.com

GOLDEN SADDLE CYCLERY
1618 Lucile Ave,
Los Angeles, CA 90026
goldensaddlecyclery.com

HELEN'S CYCLES
2501 Broadway,
Santa Monica, CA 90404
helenscycles.com

JUST RIDE LA
1626 S Hill St,
Los Angeles, CA 90015
justridela.com

LA SUCKS FOR CYCLING
instagram.com/explore/tags/
lasucksforcycling
twitter.com/hashtag/lasucks-
forcycling

MT LOWE RAILWAY TRAIL
Altadena, CA 91001
singletracks.com/bike-trails/
mount-lowe-railway

NEW PIER RIDE
facebook.com/I-enjoy-riding-
on-but-in-no-way-condone-the-
actions-of-the-New-Pier-Ride

PEDAL OR NOT
214 Pier Ave,
Santa Monica, CA 90405
pedalornot.net

ROSE BOWL RIDE
facebook.com/RoseBowlRide

SOCIAL BICYCLE
socialbicycles.com

SPOKES 'N STUFF
4730 Crystal Springs Dr,
Griffith Park, CA 90027
spokes-n-stuff.com/
griffith_park.html

TOPANGA CREEK BICYCLES
1273 N Topanga Canyon Blvd,
Topanga, CA 90290
topangacreekbicycles.com

TOUR OF CALIFORNIA
amgentourofcalifornia.com

VELO CLUB LA GRANGE
lagrange.org

VELO SPORTS CENTER
18400 Avalon Blvd,
Carson, CA 90746
lavelodrome.org

OTHER USEFUL SITES

LA METRO
metro.net

LOS ANGELES INTERNATIONAL AIRPORT
1 World Way,
Los Angeles, CA 90045
lawa.org/welcomeLAX.aspx

LYFT
lyft.com

UBER
uber.com

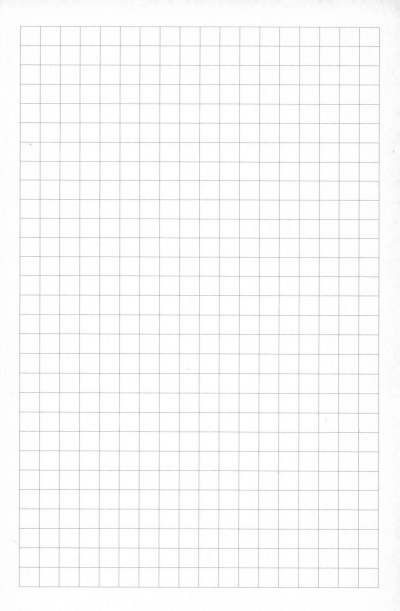

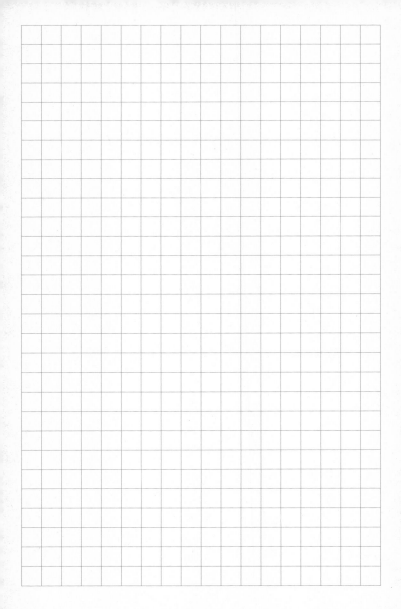

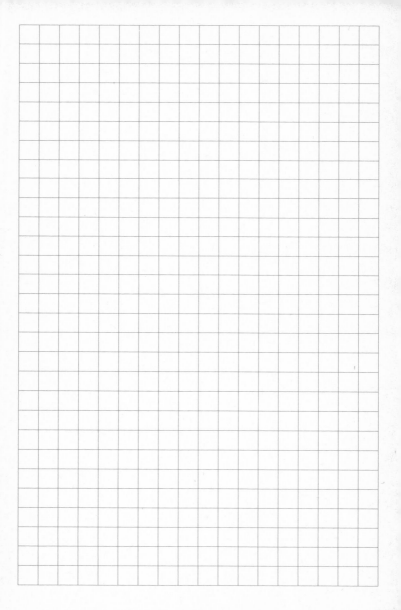

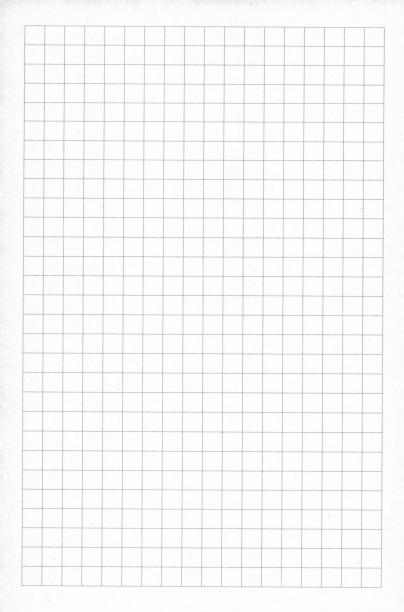

NOTES

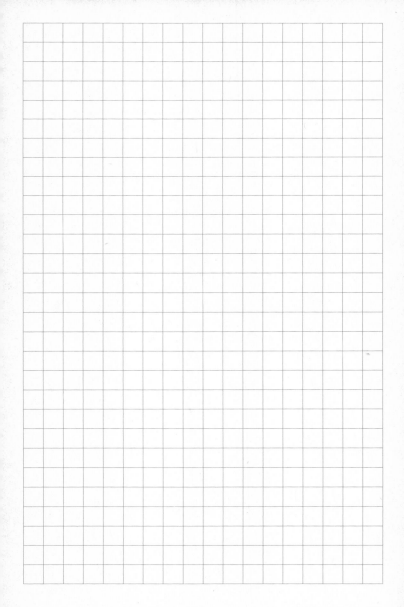

NOTES

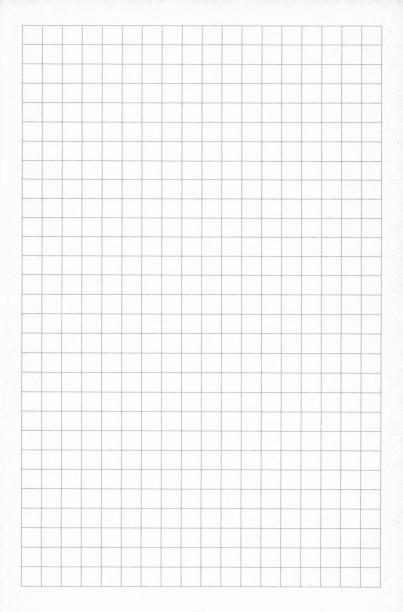

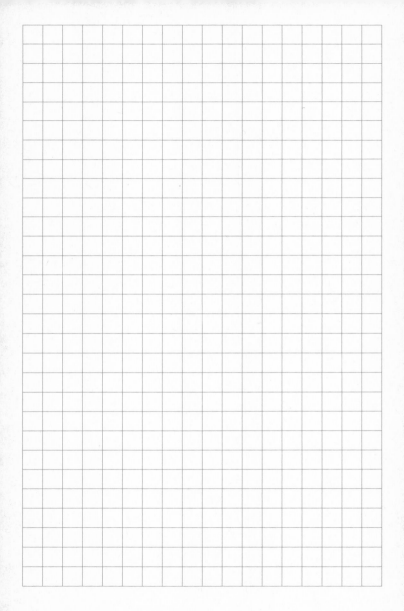

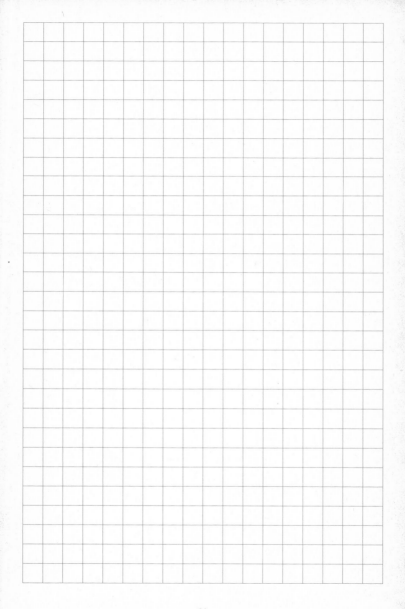

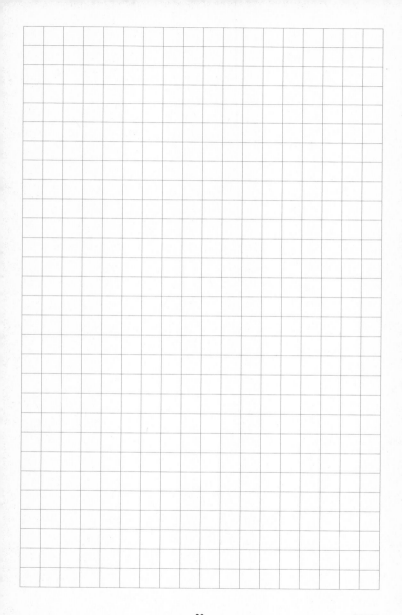

Rapha, established in London, has always been a champion of city cycling –
from testing our first prototype jackets on the backs of bike couriers, to a whole
range of products designed specifically for the demands of daily life on the bike.
As well as an online emporium of products, films, photography and stories, Rapha
has a growing network of Clubhouses, locations around the globe where cyclists
can enjoy live racing, food, drink and the latest products.

Rapha.